The White
House Kids

Rose Blue and
Corinne J. Naden

THE WHITE HOUSE KIDS

The Millbrook Press
Brookfield, Connecticut

*From Rose: To my niece Rachel Nathan,
who is full of bright ideas.*

*From Corinne: For two kids who
will soon be able to read this,
Trey Tanner and Morgan Clarey.*

Cover photograph courtesy of UPI/Bettmann
Photographs courtesy of The Bettmann Archive: pp. 16, 19, 26,
35, 40, 45, 47, 50, 53, 55, 57; The Hermitage: Home of President
Andrew Jackson, Nashville, Tenn.: p. 23; Stock Montage: p. 31;
Culver Pictures: pp. 37, 43, 48; UPI/Bettmann: pp. 60, 63, 65, 67, 71,
72, 76, 79, 81, 84; John F. Kennedy Library: p. 68 (ST-C372-6-63);
James Pickerell, Black Star: p. 75

Library of Congress Cataloging-in-Publication Data
Blue, Rose
The White House kids : children in the President's Home / by Rose
Blue and Corinne J. Naden
p.   cm.
Includes bibliographical references and index.
Summary: From Susan Adams to Chelsea Clinton, the children who
have lived in the White House are a select group. They have many
things in common; but as this book shows, their lives are very
different—at the center of exciting events, but growing up with the world
watching.
ISBN 1-56294-447-9
1. Children of presidents—United States—History—Juvenile literature.
[1. Children of presidents. 2. Presidents—Family. 3. White House
(Washington, D.C.)] I. Naden, Corinne J. II. Title
E176.45.B58 1995 973'.099—dc20   [B]   94–11293   CIP   AC

Published by The Millbrook Press
2 Old New Milford Road, Brookfield, Connecticut 06804

Contents

The White
House Kids

Introduction:
A Special Group

The White House, a beautiful old building in Washington, D.C., is the center of the United States government. The president of the United States works there, in a large room called the Oval Office. In the White House, presidents have entertained royalty, asked Congress to declare war, signed peace treaties, held press conferences, shaken hands with the winners of the Super Bowl, and even said hello to an American astronaut who was standing on the moon.

The president doesn't just work in the White House, however. He lives there, too. Every president after George Washington—a total of forty different men—has lived in the White House. Where the president lives, so does the president's family. Through the years, the president's family has often included children, some of them adopted. They are daughters and sons, grandchildren, nieces and nephews, cousins, and even family friends. Some of them lived in the president's home for several years, some for only a month. Only five presidents—Polk, Pierce, Buchanan, McKinley, and Harding—lived in the White House with no children.

George Washington never lived in the White House because it wasn't built until 1800, when the second U.S. president, John Adams, was in office. The splendid white-gray sandstone building at 1600 Pennsylvania Avenue sits on eighteen acres. Three stories high with 132 rooms, it is, as President Washington envisioned, a symbol of living history for all Americans. The White House may belong to the American people, but through the years nearly two hundred children have called it home.

Home in the White House is the Family Quarters on the second floor. These are private rooms that the public rarely gets to see. Besides the bedrooms and family sitting room, where presidents and their families can relax in private, the Family Quarters contain some famous rooms where important overnight guests often stay. These include the Lincoln Bedroom and the Queen's Room, so-called because five queens have slept there; one was England's Elizabeth II.

A child's days in the Family Quarters and in the White House don't last long. Children grow up and go away to school or move out. A U.S. president can now serve no more than eight years. Only Franklin Roosevelt has been in office longer. And some presidents don't get reelected or don't even serve a full four-year term. But through the nearly two hundred years since the White House was built, and in the lives of the forty different families that lived there, lots of ordinary, and some extraordinary, things have happened. While the queen of England has dinner downstairs, a teenager does homework upstairs. While her father is in the Oval Office worrying about war in a far-off land, a young girl scratches the ear of her pet cat. Weddings have been celebrated in the White House, babies have been born, teens have held parties, brothers have had fistfights, and some daredevils have even roller-skated down its halls.

These are the White House kids. They belong to a very special group of young people. They may do the things that children all over America do, but their lives are very different. They live in the most special home in the nation. Everyone recognizes them. Everyone recognizes their parents. People smile and wave when they ride by. They meet important people from all over the world. They don't have to take out the garbage. They travel. They ride in helicopters. They get an autographed baseball from the latest home run king. They are admired and envied.

Who wouldn't want to be a White House kid?

But think about it. Would *you*? Is living in the White House really a good deal?

Living as a White House kid is like living in a huge fishbowl. Everyone knows pretty much everything you do. If you fall off a horse and look silly, someone is bound to snap your picture and print it in the morning newspaper. If your father or mother falls off a horse and looks silly, you can be sure it will be in the morning newspaper. For your safety, Secret Service agents follow everywhere you go. That means you can count on them being around even if you're old enough to date. Everyone knows your parents, but not everyone likes them. That means you are going to hear lots of not-very-nice things said about them. And that can be hard to take.

It's not always easy growing up with the entire country watching. There are happy times, rough times, and private times that are too often public. From the children of the Founders to the present day, these young people have many stories to tell. Some of them have shared those stories with the authors of this book.

To find out what it's really like to live in a fishbowl, to find out how it changed their lives, come meet the members of this special group. Find out if you'd really like to be a White House kid.

Founding Families

CHAPTER ONE

Washington to J. Q. Adams

There were no White House kids during George Washington's two terms in office. That's because the first president of the United States is the only one who never lived in the White House. But Washington's household did include young children while he was president.

Although he had no children of his own, Washington adopted Jacky and Little Patt Custis when he married widowed Martha Dandridge Custis in 1759. Little Patt died of tuberculosis at sixteen. Jacky, who married when still a teenager, died at an early age, too, leaving behind four children. The two youngest, Nelly and Little Wash (for George Washington) Custis, went to live with their grandparents.

Nelly was ten and Little Wash was eight when their grandfather became president in 1789. They were the first children to live in a U.S. president's home, first in New York City and then in Philadelphia. Washington adored and spoiled them. Lively Nelly loved all the attention, but Little Wash had some trouble growing up as the president's grandson. He never did well in school and caused his loving grandfather much heartache before he settled down and became a successful raiser of sheep. Little Wash's only child, Mary, married Robert E. Lee, who would lead the Southern army against the North in the Civil War.

Susan Adams

The very first of the White House kids was Susan Adams, granddaughter of John Adams. The plump, brilliant, and cranky second president took over the government of the young nation in 1797. By that time, his four children—Abigail, John Quincy, Charles, and Thomas—were all grown. John Quincy would become the only child of a president also to become president.

Like Washington, Adams lived in the temporary capital of Philadelphia. The White House wasn't ready for its first First Family until November 1800. Actually, it wasn't ready then. Half of the thirty-six rooms hadn't been plastered, a wooden bridge led up to the front door, and the bathroom was in the backyard. The First Lady, Abigail Smith Adams, wrote to her daughter that nothing was finished and the whole place was "drafty."

Adams lost his run for a second term to Thomas Jefferson. Therefore, the Adams family lived in the White House only four months. During that short period, Susan became a White House kid, following the death of her father, Charles. Abigail Adams traveled to New York City to bring back her granddaughter, whom she called a "four-year-old mite in a black dress." It was the custom for even small children to wear black after a death in the family.

[14]

Losing a parent and going to a new home, even if it was the White House, understandably made Susan a difficult child. In fact, the tiny tot had a terrible temper. Once a friend, Ann Black, came to play and broke some of the dishes in Susan's prized toy tea set. Susan thought it was done on purpose. The next time she visited her friend, Susan smashed the head of Ann's doll.

The White House was probably not the best home for a child who needed lots of attention, which the president and his wife did not always have time to give. Not surprisingly, the terrible-tempered youngster grew into a terrible-tempered teenager. Her grandparents had their hands full when they all moved back to Quincy, Massachusetts, after the president's defeat. Susan lived there until she married at age sixteen, making her grandparents more unhappy than ever. Widowed soon after her daughter was born, Susan once again lived with John and Abigail Adams until her remarriage.

James Jefferson

Susan Adams was the first White House kid, but the first child actually to be born in the White House was James Jefferson, the grandson of Thomas Jefferson, our third president.

Jefferson was a widower with two grown daughters, Martha and Mary (also called Marie or Polly), when he moved into the White House in 1801. The wooden bridge still let visitors in the front door, the roof leaked, and the huge East Room, where elegant state dinners are held today, wasn't yet plastered. After Mary's death at a young age, Jefferson insisted that Martha and her

Martha Jefferson Randolf, Thomas Jefferson's daughter, brought her family to live in the White House.

family come to the White House to live. Her second son, named for James Madison, was born there. He lived until age twenty-eight and never married. In all, Martha had twelve children who lived to adulthood, but only James was born in the White House.

Jefferson was a loving grandfather. He wanted his grandchildren around him all the time. During his eight years in office, the White House was a merry scene of youngsters scampering up and down the still unfinished halls.

The Madisons

There weren't nearly as many children around when the fourth president, James Madison, took office in 1809. James and Dolley Dandridge Payne Todd Madison were a devoted couple well known for their lavish parties. Dolley had often acted as Jefferson's official hostess when he was in office. Presidents at that time, and for a long time after, did not have a staff to help them run both the business and social aspects of the presidency. It was the custom for the president's wife or other female relative to act as official hostess, in charge of state dinners and other social occasions. In the same way, a president's son often became his secretary, taking care of paperwork and business appointments for the chief of state. Today, the president has a huge White House staff to handle all business and social matters.

James and Dolley Madison did have one child, Payne Todd, a White House kid at age eighteen. A child of Dolley's first marriage, Payne was adopted by Madison when he was just three years old, and the boy called him Papa. The Madisons loved their handsome and charming son, but he was "spoiled rotten," and more of a problem than a joy. During 1812, Payne lived in the White House for six months as his stepfather's secretary. After that, he spent his time and his parents' money traveling or at the racetrack or gambling halls. Madison was forever keeping his stepson from debtor's prison. After the president's death in 1836, Dolley Madison had to sell some of her silver to get Payne out of debt once again. None of this appeared to bother him. At age sixty-one, he said on his deathbed that the only person he had harmed was "himself."

As though Payne wasn't enough of a headache, the Madisons had to deal with the near destruction of the White House in 1814. Only the outer walls remained after the British burned it during the War of 1812. The Madisons would never live there again.

The government wanted the White House rebuilt quickly. They hired James Hoban, who had designed it in the first place, to rebuild it exactly as before. The plaster was not yet dry and the floors were mostly without carpets when the fifth president, James Monroe, moved in during the fall of 1817.

Two Weddings James and Elizabeth Kortright Monroe brought with them the third White House kid. She was blond, perky Maria, age fourteen. The Monroe's other daughter, sedate, dark-haired Eliza, was many years older and already the mother of seven-year-old Hortensia when her father became president. The two sisters, so different in age and personality, did not get along.

Eliza Monroe directed social events at the White House while her father was in office.

As for their mother, Elizabeth Monroe was a snob. In great contrast to Dolley Madison, this First Lady had no intention of calling on or staging parties for the common people of Washington. Much of the White House socializing was turned over to Eliza. Largely educated in France, where her father had been a diplomat, Eliza had very strict ideas about the proper way to behave and to entertain. In a short time, she managed to offend most of the government officials in Washington because she refused to make social calls on their wives. All this fuss may seem silly, but—without television or telephones, without automobiles, motion pictures, or electricity—parties, teas, and social get-togethers were extremely important to both personal and professional life in Washington.

Eliza finally took charge of one social occasion too many. It happened to be Maria's wedding. At the age of sixteen, Maria Monroe became the first White House kid to be a White House bride. On March 9, 1820, dressed in a white gown and standing on a new rug in the Blue Room, she married Samuel Lawrence Gouverneur, age twenty-one. Unfortunately, almost no one knew about it. Low-key Eliza staged a *very* low-key wedding. There was only one party beforehand, one announcement in the newspaper, and just a few relatives and friends in attendance. Foreign diplomats were told to take no notice of the affair. That meant no gifts. It might have been a fine celebration for low-key Eliza, but not for high-spirited Maria. She never forgave her older sister.

Another wedding took place in the Blue Room during the next administration. John Quincy Adams, son of John Adams, became the sixth president of the United States in 1825. By that time, the three sons of the president and his wife, Louisa Catherine Johnson, were grown. However, son John, along with his whole senior class, was kicked out of Harvard for rioting, so he lived in the White House as his father's secretary. On February 25, 1828, John became the only son of a president to marry in the White House. Neither of his brothers would attend. That was because John married Mary Catherine Hellen, who had earlier been engaged to his older brother George. This annoyed George, who stayed away. Siding with George, the youngest brother, Charles Francis, wouldn't attend either.

The first grandchild of John Quincy and Louisa Adams was born in the White House. Named Mary Louisa, she softened the heart of her generally stern, somewhat aloof grandfather. He called her Looly and taught her to read and write.

The children of the Founding Families hold a special place in history. Some of them adjusted well to their circumstances, some didn't. They quarreled with siblings, enjoyed their popularity or struggled with it, and, in general, tried to cope with growing up, as did all those after them who joined the ranks of the White House kids.

Pre-Civil War Families

CHAPTER TWO

Jackson to Buchanan

For twelve years, the ladies and gentlemen of the nation's capital had lived with the snobbery of the Monroes and the aloofness of the unsociable President Adams. So, it must have been a shock when Andrew Jackson hit town. After the ceremonies on Inauguration Day, March 4, 1829, the seventh U.S. president rode his horse to the White House, where the "crowd hurled itself on the refreshments . . . women fainted, fights erupted—noses, clothing, and furniture were bloodied," Senator Daniel Webster said. "I have never seen such a crowd before."

Clearly, the reins of government had passed from the aristocracy of Virginia and Massachusetts. The new leader was a tough former general with the nickname of Old Hickory. Born in the frontier border of North and South Carolina, Jackson was a man of the people. His beloved wife, Rachel, had died three months before his inauguration. They had no children, although a visitor

Andrew Jackson, Jr., was the adopted son of President Andrew Jackson.

to their home at the Hermitage in Tennessee, and later in the White House, would have been surprised to learn that. Children were everywhere, most of them relatives of Rachel Robards Jackson. The Jacksons adopted one of them at birth and named him Andrew Jackson, Jr.

The White House during Jackson's eight years was a lively scene of fistfights, weddings, birthday parties, and children running up and down the halls. When his adopted son married, President Jackson pronounced his wife, Sarah, both mistress of the Hermitage and sometime-hostess at the White House.

Unhappily, Andy Jr. was a poor businessman—so poor that in later years Jackson nearly lost his beloved Hermitage to debt. Out of respect for him, the State of Tennessee bought the plantation so the former president and his family could live there. Today it is preserved as a national treasure.

Our eighth president, Martin Van Buren, was a widower. When he took office in 1837, his four sons—Abraham, John, Martin, and Smith—were grown. However, at various times through his one term, the young men lived at the White House and worked for their father. Van Buren was an elegant man with curly hair and charming manners—too charming, in the eyes of the American public, who criticized the Van Burens for their "chumminess" with British royalty and their adoption of British ways. Perhaps that is one of the reasons this president served only one term.

The youngest Van Buren son, Smith, married the niece of author Washington Irving and began to work on his father's papers. Through the years it has become customary for presidents, upon leaving office, to devote time to putting memoirs of their years in office in some order. The memoirs are usually eventually displayed in a presidential museum, such as Harry Truman's in Independence, Missouri, or Franklin Roosevelt's in Hyde Park, New York.

Our ninth president spent less time in the White House, and in office, than any other. William Henry Harrison was inaugurated on March 4, 1841. During the ceremony he stood bareheaded and coatless for hours in a bitter wind and caught a cold, which turned into pneumonia. The president died exactly one month later. Harrison and his wife, Anna Symmes, had ten children. For just one month, from Inauguration Day until Harrison's death, two of their grandsons, William Henry III and James, were White House kids.

The Tyler Clan

No one was more surprised than John Tyler to find himself suddenly the tenth president of the United States. After Harrison's inauguration, Tyler had gone back to his home in Williamsburg, Virginia, where he expected to live out his term as vice president. But at five o'clock in the morning of April 5, 1841, he received the shocking news of Harrison's death and left for Washington immediately. Not long after, he sat in the White House in front of his seven children and said, "I hope you will conduct yourselves with more than usual propriety and decorum."

By most accounts, the Tyler clan did just that, although only four of the seven were actually White House kids. The three oldest, Mary, Robert, and John Jr., were already married and living elsewhere. Because

PRESIDENT TYLER'S
PARTY FOR CHILDREN.

the president's wife was confined to a wheelchair, twenty-year-old Letitia, named for her mother, often acted as White House hostess.

The other Tyler White House kids were Elizabeth, seventeen; Alice, fourteen; and Tazewell, a shy boy of ten who was often lost in the bustle of young ladies and continuous parties during Tyler's less than four years in office. In 1844, two years after his wife died and while still president, John Tyler married Julia Gardner, who was thirty years younger than he. Much like many children today, the Tyler daughters did not adjust well to their new stepmother. Only Tazewell, surprisingly, seemed to welcome her.

In the years after the president left office, another seven Tyler children were born. In all, Tyler had fourteen children who lived to maturity, more than any other president. Eventually, Tazewell went off to California to practice medicine and was a surgeon for the South during the Civil War.

Polk to Buchanan

There were no White House kids during the four years (1845 to 1849) that James Knox Polk served as president. He and his wife, Sarah Childress, were the first presidential couple without children. The next president was Zachary Taylor. He and his wife, Margaret Mackall Smith, brought back the sounds of young voices for at least a short time when he became the nation's twelfth president in 1849. The ex-general's children were grown when he took office. Daughter Mary often served as White House hostess because her mother was chronically ill. Richard was a frail boy who was sent to Yale to become a scholar. Daughter Sarah had died at a young age. The oldest, Ann, was married with four children. Since they lived in nearby Baltimore, they were frequent visitors to the grand old mansion.

The Taylor grandchildren enjoyed only one Christmas at the White House, however. The following Fourth of July, during a heat wave, the president sat through a long celebration at the Washington Monument. He drank large quantities of ice water to beat the heat. That night he fell ill and died on July 9 of cholera, a serious infection caused by bacteria in drinking water. He had been president for less than a year and a half.

Like Tyler before him, Millard Fillmore was quite surprised to find himself president. In 1850, he and his wife, Abigail Powers, had two children, twenty-four-year-old Powers and nineteen-year-old Abbie. Young Abbie was a charming and outgoing girl who helped her ailing mother at White House parties and generally filled the president's home with laughter and activity. A talented musician, she played the harp, piano, and guitar at White House functions. Mrs. Fillmore herself was a most interesting personality. A teacher by profession, she continued to teach after her marriage, so that her husband could study law. This was unheard of in her day. She was also dismayed to discover that the White House had no books at all, not even a dictionary! Congress quickly gave the First Lady funds to buy some reading material.

The next two administrations—those of Franklin Pierce and James Buchanan—brought in another period without White House kids. Pierce and his wife, Jane Means Appleton, had one son, eleven-year-old Bennie, whom they adored. Bennie was thrilled when his father was elected president. He looked forward to April 1853, when he would celebrate his twelfth birthday in the White House. But in January, before Pierce took office, the family was involved in a train wreck, and Bennie was killed. It was a tragedy from which neither parent ever recovered.

James Buchanan was the nation's first bachelor president. He was sixty-five years old when he took office in 1857, and his niece, Harriet Lane, acted as White House hostess. As Buchanan's administration ended, the young nation was moving ever closer to war.

The Civil War and After

CHAPTER THREE

Lincoln to Arthur

Two young boys, rascals by all accounts, became White House kids in 1861. They were Willie, ten years old, and Tad, seven, the impish sons of the sixteenth president of the United States, Abraham Lincoln, and his wife, Mary Todd. Young Tad's real name was Thomas, but when his father first saw him, he said, ''He's like a little tadpole,'' and the nickname stuck. The Lincolns also had two other sons. Robert was a freshman at Harvard when his father became president, and Eddie had died before Willie was born.

The Lincolns were indulgent parents. Some said it was a wonder any of the Lincoln boys learned to walk, because their father was forever carrying them around. Indeed, the president took great delight in his children and seemed never to mind when Tad burst into the White House office to give his father a hug. Tad also shot his toy cannon at the door in the middle of a Cabinet meeting. He set up a refreshment stand on the

White House lawn to raise money for charity, and made sure that visiting dignitaries bought something. Official guests were sometimes startled to find themselves sitting next to Tad or Willie at a state dinner, and it was rumored that a pet goat was once seen resting on Tad's bed.

Even if only half the stories were true, Tad Lincoln obviously enjoyed being a White House kid. Willie was a little more sedate and, unfortunately, died of a fever before his twelfth birthday. Although the president was shattered by the death of his beloved son, he coped with the loss far better than did his wife. Mrs. Lincoln could never accept the loss, and her physical and emotional health declined.

Through all the ups and downs of family life, Lincoln and the country wrestled with the horror and tragedy of the Civil War. He won reelection in 1864, and the South surrendered the following year. Soon after, on April 14, Lincoln was assassinated by John Wilkes Booth while attending Ford's Theatre in Washington, D.C. His beloved Tad lived only until age eighteen, when he died of pneumonia. Mary Todd Lincoln was committed to a hospital for the insane where she remained for some time. After she was released, she lived in France until shortly before her death in 1882.

The Johnsons

Andrew Johnson became the third U.S. president thrust suddenly into power. When he and his wife, Eliza McCardle, moved in after Lincoln's death, the White House staff thought it had another mischief maker in Andrew Johnson, Jr., who, for some unknown reason, was called Frank. But the twelve-year-old boy was quiet and well-mannered. Like Tazewell Tyler some years before him, Frank Johnson seemed lost in the jumble and bustle of a White House filled with parties and receptions.

The rest of the family—two sons, two daughters, and five grandchildren—all moved to Washington. Son Robert became his father's secretary, and daughter Martha, with help from her sister Mary, took over as hostess for their ailing mother. The whole family's attitude toward their new status is perhaps best described by Martha, who declared, ''We are plain people from Tennessee. I hope too much will not be expected of us.''

However, the Johnson grandchildren, who ranged in age from ten to five, had no fears about people's expectations. They loved the White House spotlight. They took dance lessons as well as piano and violin, and the stately old house was usually filled with music and laughter. During all the commotion, the White House was being renovated—after a fashion. Mrs. Johnson decided that repairs and redecorating cost too much money, so she launched a do-it-yourself project, mending old pieces of furniture and shopping for bargains to replace worn pieces.

The Grants

One son in the next White House family possibly spent more time on the president's home than in it. Eleven-year-old Jesse Root Grant, a budding astronomer, loved the White House roof. He was one of four children of the nation's eighteenth president, Ulysses Simpson Grant, and his wife, Julia Dent. The others were Frederick, nineteen; U.S. Jr. (called Buck), sixteen; and Nellie, thirteen.

Soon after the former Civil War general took office in 1869, Jesse installed his small, powerful telescope on the White House roof. When the president had time, he joined his son and they charted the heavens until Mrs. Grant made them come down. Besides stargazing, Jesse

Opposite:
Nellie Grant's
White House
wedding was
an elegant
affair.

enjoyed riding one of his two ponies around Washington every day.

The Grants called their children "the best and smartest in the world" and treated them accordingly. In time, both Nellie and Jesse were sent away to school. When they each wrote to their father saying they were too homesick to stay, the president told them to come back to the White House.

Nellie was married in 1874 in the most lavish wedding the White House had ever seen. The East Room was decorated with a huge wedding bell of white roses. The president was not happy, however, because his beloved daughter married an Englishman and went to Europe. When the marriage failed, however, she returned to the United States and eventually remarried. Jesse the astronomer went out West and set up a gambling casino. He must have remembered his youth with pleasure, for he later wrote that "the White House was the largest and best playground available."

The Hayes Children

When Rutherford B. Hayes became the nation's nineteenth president in 1877, his seventeen-year-old son, Ruddy, was away at school. Whenever the young man came home, he complained that he couldn't find a bed and that there were people sleeping in bathtubs because the White House was so crowded.

Ruddy may have been right. If so, the reason was the First Lady. Lucy Webb Hayes was beautiful, outgoing, and the first wife of a president to be a true college graduate. She loved people and parties, and the White

[34]

House was always full of both. There were Easter-egg rolls on the lawn, hosted by the youngest Hayes children, nine-year-old Fanny and six-year-old Scott. These two had a fine time. They learned to ride horses, went to dancing school, and played the piano and sang for guests.

Hayes and his wife had two older children. Birchard, twenty-three, was building a law practice in Ohio, and Webb, twenty-one, had recently graduated from Cornell and worked as his father's secretary. Of all his children, the president regarded Webb as "not scholarly." Yet it was this White House kid who left his father the most lasting tribute. In his father's memory, Webb established the first of the presidential libraries at Fremont, Ohio.

The Garfields

The next administration brought in five new White House kids, if only for a short time. James Abram Garfield, twentieth president of the United States, took office in March 1881 and died that September.

When Garfield and his wife, Lucretia Rudolph, moved into the White House, so did Hal, seventeen; Jim, sixteen; Mollie, fourteen; Irvin McDowell, ten; and Abram, eight. The Garfields were a close, loving family. The president's mother was often at the White House, too, and she was the first presidential mother to attend her son's inauguration. The two oldest Garfield children were supposed to be away at school when their father took office, but they were allowed to live in the White House and take lessons from a tutor until entering Williams College that fall.

Opposite: The five Garfield children lived in the White House for less than a year.

[36]

The two youngest Garfields, Irwin and Abram, were more interested in riding their bicycles up and down the White House halls than in study. A new tennis court was laid out on the lawn, and the president often joined in a lively game with his sons. Young Mollie was a pretty girl who played the piano and loved to entertain her friends at lunch.

Life for these White House kids, however, was not all fun. Like other families before and after them, the Garfield children soon learned that their father had little private time. The family did not have breakfast together for a period of twenty-two weeks. At one time, Hal decided he was in love and wanted to have a private talk with his father. However, he couldn't get an appointment and had to wait a month to see the president alone. Hal never did marry the girl.

Even though the president had little time for them, Garfield loved his children and was very concerned that they have a proper education. He was so strict about learning that they called him the "General." Young Mollie was often seen, books in hand, skipping alone on the streets of Washington on her way to school. As yet, no one thought that White House kids needed to be protected from the public.

However, it was not the Garfield children but the father who needed protection. On July 2, the president set out for the railroad station to join his family for a summer vacation. He was shot twice in the back by a mentally ill man, Charles J. Guiteau. At first, doctors thought that Garfield would live. He was sent to the New

Jersey seashore to recover, but he died on September 19, 1881. He was the second U.S. president to be assassinated.

Gone were the warm, loving family days in the White House. Eventually, Hal, Jim, and Irvin Garfield became attorneys, and Abram an architect. Mollie married her father's private secretary, and she and brother Hal had a double wedding.

For the fourth time in the nation's young history, a surprised vice president took office to complete a deceased president's term. He was Chester Alan Arthur, a widower with two children, Alan and Nellie.

The Arthurs

Seventeen-year-old Alan Arthur, a student at Princeton, was thrilled to suddenly discover that his home address was the White House! As often as he could, he rushed home from school to entertain his friends at his new address. He was especially pleased to borrow the presidential carriage. It was a stylish dark-green vehicle drawn by two fine horses. Alan thought he made quite an impression on the young ladies of Washington as he drove the carriage about town.

His father wasn't so pleased, however. Chester Alan Arthur, twenty-first president of the United States, was extremely concerned about the welfare of his children. Like more modern presidents, he was very careful about keeping them out of the public eye, but he was afraid that the glitter of the White House was turning Alan into a playboy. Nine-year-old Nellie was far less of a worry. She attended nearly all the White House receptions.

In this rare
photograph,
Nellie Arthur
wears a fur-
trimmed coat
with matching
hat and muff.

Nellie was cared for by a governess and sometimes by the president's sister, who, with her own two daughters, spent a lot of time in the president's home.

Arthur would allow no photographs of his children and no press interviews. Actually, he very nearly did not even allow them to live in the White House at all. A tall, handsome man and an elegant dresser, the new president appreciated fine things. He was so offended by the condition of the White House that he refused to move in until it was redecorated. "I will not live in a house like this," he declared.

With the approval of Congress, the White House was redone to the president's elegant standards. Arthur was so pleased that he gave a reception for five thousand people. Both White House kids attended. Nellie wore a white embroidered frock with a colored sash, which was very fashionable for little girls of the time. Alan, of course, was home from Princeton.

The president may have been right to be concerned about his son. In later years, Alan Arthur sported around the country and Europe, married twice, and became a well-known polo player. Little Nellie married Charles Pinkerton and moved to Mount Kisco, New York.

The century was ending, the country was growing up, and the White House was more and more becoming what Washington had intended, a symbol of pride to the American people. As the administrations changed, so did the faces of the youngsters who would add their names to that select group known as White House kids.

The Turn
of the Century

CHAPTER FOUR

Cleveland to Taft

In a strange quirk of American politics, the twenty-second president of the United States was also the twenty-fourth. Grover Cleveland served two separated terms, 1885 to 1889 and 1893 to 1897, the only president to do so. During his first term, forty-nine-year-old Cleveland became the only president to marry in the White House. Twenty-one-year-old Frances Folsom, called Frank, daughter of his former law partner, became his bride in 1886.

White House Babies

Three years later, Cleveland lost his party's nomination for reelection, and Benjamin Harrison became the twenty-third president. When Harrison took office in 1889, his wife, Caroline Scott, was concerned about sleeping quarters. Their own children, Russell and Mary Scott, were married, but they were often at the White House, as were the First Lady's father and Mary's two children, Mary and Benjamin, who was called Baby McKee.

Benjamin
Harrison
bounces Baby
McKee on
his knee.

About this time, cameras were coming into general use, and they certainly were used in the White House. The sounds of clicking could be heard everywhere that Baby McKee crawled—into the conference room, where he once stole some presidential papers; out on the lawn being chased by Whiskers, the family's pet goat; or in his high chair as the center of attention.

Mrs. Harrison died of cancer in 1892. Three years later, Harrison, now out of office, married his first wife's niece. His children never forgave him.

The Clevelands were back in the White House in 1893, this time bringing with them seventeen-month-old Ruth. She became the delight of all visitors to the mansion. And there were lots of visitors, indeed, for Cleveland felt, as had Washington, that the "White House belongs to the nation." He thought everyone had a right to come in. Many people did, and baby Ruth was passed among so many strangers that one morning no one could find her. The child was located without harm, but that put an end to the constant stream of guests. Unfortunately, the closed-door policy created the rumor that something was wrong with Ruth. Although it was not true, the rumor caused many heartaches for the parents of this young White House kid, who would die suddenly of diphtheria at age twelve.

Before the second term ended, two more White House kids joined the Cleveland family. They were Esther, the only child of a president ever to be born in the White House, and Marion, born at the Cleveland's summer home in Massachusetts. Everyone adored the Cleveland girls and they were frequently in the news. Two

Opposite:
Grover Cleveland and his family posed for this picture at their home in Princeton, New Jersey, in 1907.

sons also joined the family, after the end of the second term.

In her later years, Esther Cleveland, who married an Englishman and lived in Great Britain, was asked about her White House memories. She recalled sitting alone in the downstairs hall putting on a pair of gloves. The occasion was moving day. Why was she moving? "Because McKinley's coming," she said, "and there can't be two presidents."

If you're a White House kid, there is almost sure to be a moving day.

Out went Cleveland in 1897 and in came William McKinley, but no children came with him. McKinley and his wife, Ida Saxton, had two daughters who died before he became the nation's twenty-fifth president. Reelected to a second term, McKinley was the third U.S. president to be assassinated, shot by Leon Czolgosz in Buffalo, New York, on September 6, 1901. He died eight days later.

After McKinley's death, the U.S. government decided to tighten its security measures. The Secret Service, a branch of the Treasury Department established in 1865 to stop counterfeiting, was now assigned to guard the president. Today the Secret Service guards the president and vice president, their families, and presidential candidates as well.

The Six Roosevelts

Once again, a surprised vice president and his family found themselves in the White House. They were Theodore Roosevelt, his wife, Edith Carow, and the six chil-

Theodore Roosevelt's six children turned the White House upside down.

dren: Alice, seventeen and the daughter of the president's first wife, who had died in 1884; Ted, fourteen; Kermit, twelve; Ethel, ten; Archibald, seven; and Quentin, three.

What a wild place the White House became! The quiet and sedate McKinley years turned into Roosevelt mania. Beautiful, lively Alice, who adored her stepmother, was the country's darling. She was seen at every party and was considered quite daring. She once

Archie
and Quentin
answer
morning roll
call with the
White House
policemen.

brought her pet snake, named Emily Spinach, with her when calling on a friend. Complaints reached the president's ears that Alice hung out with friends who "drove too fast." When asked why he couldn't make his oldest child behave a little better, Roosevelt replied, "I can be president or I can supervise Alice. Nobody could do both."

In the meantime, the younger White House kids were enjoying the president's house, too. Ethel, terrific at all sports, was known as the White House tomboy. She and brother Kermit were especially close. They often followed the lamplighter in the streets around the White House, putting out the lights nearly as fast as he turned them on. They walked on stilts through the hallways and skated on the polished floors. When one of the children had the measles, the others took their pet pony up in the elevator for a visit. Quentin and his friends were caught throwing spitballs at the portrait of Andrew Jackson; his father gave him a stern lecture. A pet kangaroo rat ate sugar on the breakfast table, and a small figure was sure to be seen shimmying up the flagpole each day.

In all its history, the White House probably has never seen such chaos and merriment. Roosevelt served two terms, and, of course, the White House kids grew up and went about their lives.

After traveling around the country and the world, Alice married Representative Nicholas Longworth of Ohio in 1906. The White House wedding rivaled that of Nellie Grant. Actually, Nellie Grant Sartoris was a wedding guest! Ted served in World War I and lost his life in the invasion of Normandy during World War II. Kermit died in the Aleutian Islands during World War II. Ethel married Dr. Richard Derby and joined him in the American Ambulance Corps during World War I. Archie was seriously wounded in World War I and also served in World War II in the Pacific. Quentin lost his life at the age of twenty in France during World War I.

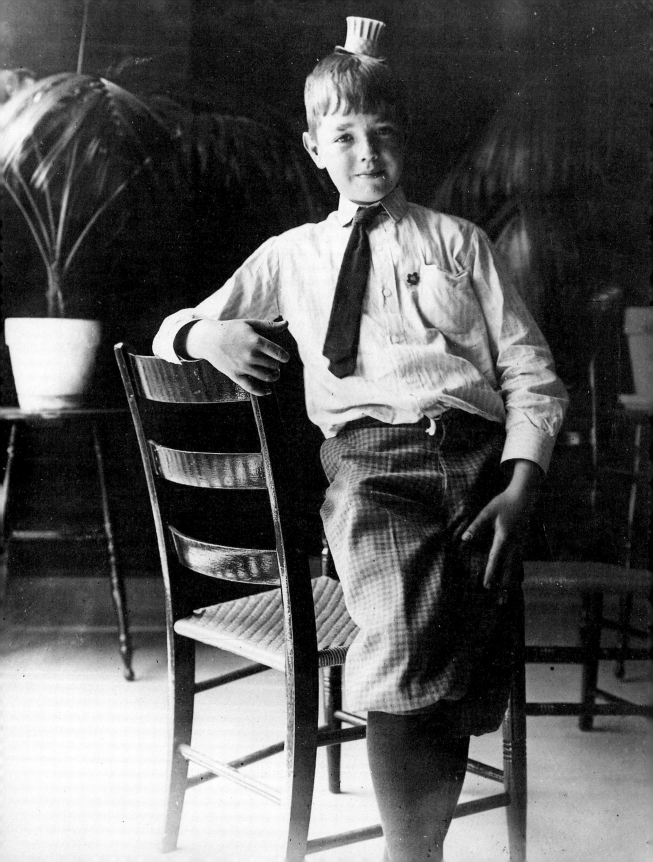

The Tafts

When William Howard Taft took office in 1909, all three of his children attended the inaugural. Only one, however, actually lived in the White House. Robert was at Yale and Helen at Bryn Mawr, where she later became dean. Robert became a U.S. senator from Ohio, and the Taft family name remains one of the most prominent in American political life.

Fun-loving, handsome, and studious Charlie, twelve years old, sat through his father's inaugural ceremony clutching a copy of *Treasure Island.* He took it along in case he "got bored." The twenty-seventh president later called it a great compliment that Charlie never opened the book.

The Taft White House may not have been as boisterous a place as the Roosevelt White House, but William Taft was said to be the most jovial of all American presidents. He was certainly the largest, tipping the scales, at times, at well over 300 pounds! The Taft White House was also greatly subdued and saddened when, three months into the term, the president's wife, Helen Herron Taft, had a paralyzing stroke. Daughter Helen came home from school to help out as hostess during her mother's long recovery.

Times were changing at the White House. Taft was the first U.S. president to ride around in an automobile and the last to let a pet goat graze on the lawn. During his administration, the cherry trees that are now a symbol of the nation's capital in spring began to flourish along the Potomac River. Their fragrant beauty was in great contrast to the war clouds that would begin to gather after the next president took office.

Opposite: Charlie Taft wears knickers and an "Uncle Sam" hat in this informal photograph.

[51]

Growing Up in a
Growing America

CHAPTER FIVE

Wilson to Johnson

When Woodrow Wilson took office in March 1913, his daughter Eleanor, twenty-three years old, crawled under her bed and cried, "It will kill them. It will kill them both." Eleanor was afraid that the pressures of the office would be too hard on her parents, who she felt were more suited to academic life. Wilson had earlier been president of Princeton University. Eleanor also feared for herself. She faced the problem that many kids of celebrities still face. Do my new friends like me because my father or mother is famous? Do my old friends avoid me because my father or mother is famous? She found it difficult to find dates because of her famous father. Some young men were scared off by the president. Others wanted to date Eleanor just to be near the seat of power. Eventually, she married her father's secretary of the treasury, a man much older than she. The simple wedding took place in the White House.

The Wilsons' other two daughters were also grown when the twenty-eighth president took office. Jessie,

Ellen and Woodrow Wilson with their daughters, Margaret, Eleanor, and Jesse.

twenty-five, visited the White House on weekends from her job in a Philadelphia settlement house. She was also married in the White House. Margaret, the youngest, spent most of her time in New York, where she studied singing.

As it turned out, Eleanor had reason to worry, for the Wilson White House years were beset with problems.

The president's wife, Ellen Axson, died in 1914. Wilson married Edith Bolling Galt the following year, and he suffered a severe stroke in 1919. He was awarded the Nobel Peace Prize in 1920 and died in 1924.

The Coolidge Boys

Warren Gamaliel Harding, president from 1921 to 1923, and his wife, Florence Kling DeWolfe, had no children. When Harding died in San Francisco after an exhausting cross-country speaking tour, Calvin Coolidge became the sixth vice president to take office on the death of a president. He and his wife, Grace Anna Goodhue, moved in, and the White House once again was filled with teenage pranks and laughter. Seventeen-year-old John and fifteen-year-old Calvin Jr. attended boarding school during those years (1923 to 1929), but they were very often at home.

"Things were different in Washington in those days," said John Coolidge in an interview for this book. "During the summers, the town closed down, even Congress, due to the beastly heat. There was no air conditioning then."

John and his brother were very close. The whole family was devastated during the summer of 1924 when young Calvin, the more devilish of the two boys, died of an infection. It developed after Calvin played tennis barefoot on the White House courts.

Stern, quiet, uncommunicative President Coolidge wept at his son's funeral. Said John, "Calvin was my father's favorite. It hurt him terribly. It hurt us all."

During their short time together in the White House, John remembers how he and his brother loved

[54]

The Coolidge boys, John (right) and Calvin Jr., relax at the edge of the Tidal Basin in Washington, D.C.

to ride horses. "There was a beautiful bridle path on the White House grounds," he said. "My horse was named Captain. An army post was near the White House and we sometimes rode those horses."

When asked about living in the spotlight, John replied, "The president had more privacy then than he does now. Without TV, he wasn't so recognizable, so he could wander about usually unnoticed. My father enjoyed window shopping, and the Secret Service was not readily identified either."

Somebody must have seen the Secret Service, however, because it was widely joked that the only way John would ever marry was to elope and avoid the Secret Service agent who followed him. He didn't elope, but he did marry Florence Trumbull after his father left office.

John Coolidge never felt comfortable with the formality of living in the White House. He preferred casual dress but was told by his father, "This is the president's house. You dress for dinner and arrive promptly." John did both.

The Hoover Grandchildren

Peggy Brigham also has lots of memories of being a White House kid, as the granddaughter of Herbert Hoover, thirty-first president of the United States. Hoover had two sons, Allan and Herbert Jr. Allan, the youngest, found the White House boring, said it gave him "the willies," and headed for a career in business. Herbert Jr., an engineer, was the father of Peggy Brigham.

In an interview for this book, Peggy Brigham talked about the White House years. Her father was recuperating from tuberculosis in a sanatorium, so Peggy, her mother, brother Herbert III (Peter), and sister Joan Leslie moved into the White House with her grandparents.

"We were on the top floor," Peggy said. "Windows opened onto the lawn where we watched the autogyro [a helicopter] land. I also remember the Easter egg

Opposite: Herbert Hoover III and Peggy Anne greet visitors to the White House Easter egg roll in 1931. First Lady Lou Henry Hoover is on the right.

hunt on the south lawn. I played around the trees on the lawn and, because I was little and near the ground, I imagined they were my tree house. The rooms were between the roots of the trees.''

Peggy's brother didn't get as many headlines as Peggy did, probably because he was small and very well-behaved. According to one story, however, he once escaped from his nurse and was discovered standing nude in front of an upstairs window waving to people on the street.

To young Peggy, her grandparents—and especially her grandfather—were a great comfort. ''I didn't really realize who they were. They were just my grandparents. Grandpa played with me and took me places. I remember trips to the country with him, where I caught my first fish.''

Peggy recalled, ''The lack of privacy isn't as bad when you're young.'' But when they live in the White House, even young children must eventually face reality. Peggy's ''grandpa'' was in trouble with the nation. Hoover was caught in the Great Depression, the country's worst economic disaster, which began with the crash of the stock market in 1929. A great many Americans lost their jobs, their homes, and their hopes for the future. With misery everywhere, someone had to take the blame. It fell, rightly or wrongly, on the president's shoulders, and that affected his grandchildren.

''When people know who you are, you can no longer be yourself,'' Peggy said. ''A classmate once told me that she couldn't play with me any longer because, according to her mother, the Depression was my fault.

"As we grew up, our grandfather's unpopularity was harder on my brother than on me because of his last name. I remember being especially happy to be married so that my name changed."

Living in the White House sometimes means there's nowhere to hide.

FDR's Grandchildren

In 1933, a new president came in. With him came new hope and new White House kids. The thirty-second president of the United States was Franklin Delano Roosevelt. He told the people of the depression-ridden nation that they had nothing to fear "but fear itself." He would be reelected three times and would serve longer than any other American president. Unless there is a change to the U.S. Constitution, that record will not be broken. The Twenty-Second Amendment, ratified in 1951, now limits a president to two four-year terms.

Franklin and Anna Eleanor Roosevelt had five children, Anna, James, Elliot, Franklin, and John. The three oldest were married and the two youngest were at school, so none of them lived in the White House. They all complained that they rarely got to see their father once he became president. In fact, once when John did come to visit, the guards refused to let him enter. He went to a local drugstore, phoned the White House, and asked someone to let him in.

In contrast to the children, much public attention was focused on the Roosevelt grandchildren. When Anna's marriage to Curtis Dall broke up, she and her children moved in with her parents. Eleanor, six years old, and Curtis Jr., three years old, became White House

Sistie and Buzzie ride with their grandfather, Franklin D. Roosevelt, and mother, Anna Roosevelt Dall.

kids. Known as Sistie and Buzzie, they were constantly in the news. There were often pictures in the newspapers of Grandma Eleanor reading to them or hosting a party for them. Said Curtis, "It was as if we were child movie stars."

In a way, the lives of these White House kids were as unreal as a motion picture set. Curtis remembers it as a time of "tinsel and unreality," with a staff of servants always hovering nearby and meals served by a butler. He feels that being a celebrity at such a young age deeply affected his adult life.

Sistie, now known as Eleanor Roosevelt Seagraves, thinks so, too. In an interview for this book, she said, "Having been a White House kid affects you later in life." Echoing President Hoover's granddaughter, she continued, "Our youth might have affected my brother more because my name changed when I married." She and her brother dropped their last name, Dall, because they disliked their father, and they used the Roosevelt name instead. "But it was especially hard on Curtis," noted Eleanor, acknowledging that not everyone liked her grandfather. "Whether you're proud or people make you feel ashamed, the name is a label forever." That feeling is echoed by many White House kids.

In general, however, Eleanor has happy, warm memories of her young years. "At seven, you're glad to be with your grandparents when bad things happen," she said, referring to her parents' separation. "It doesn't matter if it's the White House or a row house."

The White House to young Eleanor was "a perfectly natural place to be." She said, "Things were calmer before wartime, despite the Depression. We went to private school but with less security than now or after the war. The security problem is much greater today. I really had a good time in school with lots of friends. I especially remember the fun of going to light the White House Christmas tree."

When the White House grandkids were still young, their mother married John Boettinger. The United States entered World War II in 1941, and many of the Roosevelt family, including Boettinger, went off to war. Anna returned once more to the White House with her young son Johnny. By this time, Sistie and Buzzie were in boarding school.

Being a White House kid was very different for Johnny than it had been for his half brother and half sister. The whole nation, and especially his grandfather, was preoccupied with the war. There were few parties and little entertainment at the White House. There were no children to play with, and nobody had much time for the small boy.

Franklin Roosevelt died in Warm Springs, Georgia, in April 1945, shortly before the end of the war. Harry S. Truman became the seventh U.S. vice president to fill a president's term. He and his wife, Elizabeth Wallace—known to the country as Bess—had one daughter, Margaret. She was a twenty-one-year-old college junior when her father took office, and she was aware of stepping into a fishbowl. Said Margaret later, "It was at that time I ceased to be a free agent. Never again would I open a door without knowing who was outside."

The Trumans

Truman was the nation's thirty-third president, from 1945 until 1953. But from 1949 until March 1952, the Trumans were not a White House family. They lived across the street while the White House was undergoing a renovation that transformed the grand old mansion into the building that looked much as it does today.

[62]

Harry S.
Truman and
daughter Margaret
at the piano.

Like Allan Hoover years before, Margaret Truman did not like living in the White House, even though she recalls such fun times as having watermelon seed fights with her father in the private dining room. "I can't wait to get out of here," she once said. Nonetheless, she helped her mother entertain dignitaries and tried to adjust to living in the spotlight. It wasn't easy. One time she had some unwelcome publicity because her father loudly objected when newspaper reporters criticized Margaret's singing. She did admit, however, that sometimes "the White House was interesting because of the people that I met. I became quite close to Winston Churchill."

Like her father, Margaret Truman was a down-to-earth person. She had to put up with being constantly shadowed by the Secret Service and saying goodnight to her dates under the White House floodlights. "That was not my idea of romance," she admitted.

Margaret weathered the White House years in good grace, however. After she graduated from college, she pursued a musical career, married journalist Clifton Daniel, had four sons, and is today a well-known writer of mystery novels. But she still doesn't like to see the White House, mostly because of the tight security. When her father was president, the gates were open and Truman enjoyed a daily walk. The assassination of John F. Kennedy and attempts on the lives of other presidents have caused security to be tightened immensely. To Margaret Truman Daniel, today the White House "looks like a fortress."

More Grandchildren

No kids actually lived in the White House during the next administration. John Sheldon Doud Eisenhower, the only child of General Dwight David and Mamie Doud Eisenhower, was already in the army when his father took office in 1953. However, John's children— Dwight David, Barbara Anne, and Susan Elaine—were frequently at their grandparents' home. Swings, tricy-

cles, and toys littered the White House halls and lawn. The Eisenhowers adored their grandchildren. The presidential yacht was called *Barbara Anne* and the president's weekend retreat in the Virginia hills was named, and still is, Camp David.

Young David and his grandfather were especially close. The boy followed the president around the White House grounds and often had his picture taken with him. He had an electric car, which was a very high-tech toy at the time, and loved to race around the White House halls with it. It was surprising that his grand-

[65]

mother indulged him in this because Mamie Eisenhower was persistent about keeping everything neat in the president's home. But to young David, the White House was a marvelous place to play, mostly because of the room on the top floor where he played with his toy soldiers. Because there was so much space in the White House, David never had to put away his soldiers when he was through playing with them. He just left them there and closed the door until the next day.

David Eisenhower seemed to enjoy the spotlight as much as his sister Barbara Anne did not. "It was as if I were living in a fishbowl," she said, "but when I stayed at the White House, I truly thought of the place as mine." David Eisenhower, grandson of the thirty-fourth president, would grow up to marry Julie Nixon, daughter of the thirty-seventh president. One of the things they had in common was their years as White House kids.

The Kennedy Kids

It had been many years since very young children of a president lived in the White House. That changed in 1961 when John Fitzgerald Kennedy became the thirty-fifth president. With him and his wife, Jacqueline Lee Bouvier, their three-year-old Caroline and two-month-old John-John came to the White House. Suddenly the newspapers were filled with photos and stories about the two adorable children and their antics.

The Kennedys tried to keep these White House kids out of the spotlight, but it was nearly an impossible task. There was Caroline crawling between her father's legs at his press conference or riding her pony, called Mac-

aroni. There were pictures of her in her mother's high-heeled shoes or wearing a toy six-gun strapped to her waist. Her Secret Service guard was instructed to stay far enough away to let the child play her games, and Caroline came to regard him as just another grown-up playmate.

In time, there was brother John-John peeking out from under his father's desk in the Oval Office. Sometimes the president would call his name as the child played on the south lawn, and John-John would come running. Tree houses and swings and pets adorned the White House grounds. Never had the old mansion seemed less like a national symbol and more like a fun-filled family home.

The fun ended soon enough. The Kennedy's new baby, Patrick, died two days after birth. And on November 22, 1963, after less than three years in office, the president was assassinated in Dallas, Texas.

After his death, Jacqueline Kennedy largely succeeded in raising her two children out of the constant glare of the spotlight. Caroline became a lawyer, married, and had three children of her own. John Jr. became an attorney in New York City. They continued to avoid publicity and rarely gave interviews. However, in 1992, Caroline and John Jr. were interviewed on the TV program *Prime Time Live*. They spoke of their memories of thirty years before. John remembered that his father fed him chewing gum when he hid under the desk. Caroline talked about waiting for the helicopter to land when their father returned from the nation's business. When the interviewer asked her how she managed to keep her private life so private, she replied, "Well, I haven't talked to people like you very much."

Shortly after Kennedy's death in Dallas in 1963, a shocked nation watched Lyndon B. Johnson take the oath of office as the thirty-sixth president of the United States. He was the eighth vice president to fill an unexpired term.

The Johnson Girls

The president and his wife, Claudia Taylor, known as Lady Bird, had two teenage daughters. "Let's face it," said the younger of the two when she moved into the White House on December 7, 1963, "I'll never be just Luci Johnson again." Of course, sixteen-year-old Luci Baines Johnson was right. Besides coping with the sudden spotlight, Luci was suffering through the usual insecurities of adolescence. She felt that her parents didn't understand her and that she wasn't as tall or as beautiful as her older sister, Lynda Bird, then a student at the University of Texas and on the honor roll. Luci's grades, in comparison, were poor, until it was discovered that she had vision problems. This was corrected and she became the voluntary chairman of Volunteers for Vision and spent her summers working for the cause of testing young children for possible vision problems.

Today, Luci has mixed feelings about being a White House kid. "You're a witness to history," she says, "but you're removed from your peers." More outgoing than her sister, Luci enjoyed parties and dancing. Insiders at the White House called her "Watusi Luci," after a dance that was popular at the time. Others called her "irresponsible and irresistible," mostly because of her constant efforts to avoid her Secret Service guards. In fact, Luci Johnson was just being a teenager, doing the things that teenagers do, but she had to do them in the national spotlight. She discovered what many other White House kids and children of celebrities know: When you have a famous parent, it tends to cramp your style.

Luci Johnson also did what many young people have done to escape a too-confining situation—not always with good results. She got married. In 1966, at the age of nineteen, she became the wife of Patrick Nugent and the seventh daughter of a president to be married while living in the White House. One of the guests was eighty-two-year-old Alice Roosevelt Longworth, the toast of Washington some sixty years earlier.

[71]

Less than two years later, Luci moved back into the White House. Her military husband had gone to Vietnam, the Southeast Asian land where the United States was aiding the South Vietnamese in their fight against North Vietnam. People were protesting the increasing American involvement in the war, for which they blamed the president. Luci remembers being upset by the chants outside her window of "LBJ, LBJ, how many kids did you kill today?'' Luci's son, Lyndon, became a White House kid. "Grandchildren are a great White House tonic," she said. Luci later divorced her first husband and remarried.

For a while, older sister Lynda took the headlines when she dated screen actor George Hamilton. Being a White House kid was definitely a handicap when dating, she admitted. Later, she married Marine Captain Charles Robb in another White House wedding. Now the parents of three daughters, Lynda and her husband live in Virginia, but not entirely out of the spotlight; Robb became a U.S. senator.

After Kennedy's assassination and the controversy over Vietnam that nearly tore the country apart, kids in the White House faced more tension and tighter security than ever before. They also lived in a smaller fishbowl, for television and the electronic age brought their every deed—silly or serious, bad or good—before the always-interested but rarely sympathetic public eye.

Late-Twentieth-Century Kids

CHAPTER SIX

Nixon to Clinton

Like the Johnson family, Richard Nixon and his wife Thelma Ryan (known as Pat) also had two daughters. When the thirty-seventh president took office in 1969, quiet, petite Tricia was twenty-three years old, and outgoing Julie was twenty.

Tricia kept a low profile in and out of the White House. However, she got a lot of attention in 1971 when she married lawyer Edward Cox in the first wedding ever held in the White House Rose Garden. Today, she and her husband live in New York City with their teenage son, Christopher.

In December 1968, Julie had married David Eisenhower. She wanted nothing to do with a White House wedding, and the ceremony was held in New York City shortly before her father's inauguration. Julie and David did not want their special day—the wedding of two White House kids—turned into a media circus.

Opposite: On the White House lawn, Julie introduces a group of visiting children to the Nixon family dogs.

In an interview for this book, Julie Nixon Eisenhower remembered being at the White House as a young married woman. "Some of it was fun," she said. "They put in a pool table. David and I and our friends played sardines—a hiding game—with eight to ten people on the second and third floors. The best place by far to hide was the shower in the Lincoln bedroom!" Julie's most vivid White House memory is of Thanksgiving 1969, when her father invited wounded Vietnam war veterans to dinner in the State Dining Room. A cease-fire ended American involvement in the war in Vietnam in 1973.

Today, Julie, David, and their three children live in Berwyn, Pennsylvania, where she is an author, lecturer, and volunteer. She has written a book on the life of her mother, Pat, who died in 1993. David published a biography of his famous grandfather in 1986.

Would either of the Eisenhowers try politics? "I can't rule it out," Julie said, although she worries about how this would affect her own children. "It's almost easier to be a politician than a member of the [politician's] family," she said.

Troubled Times

The Nixon daughters, and the Johnsons, too, know how difficult it is to be a member of a politician's family when there is trouble. During Lyndon Johnson's administration, public unrest and hostility had grown over the Vietnam war. Nixon faced even greater troubles. After a break-in at Democratic headquarters in Washington, D.C., officials in his administration were indicted on charges of covering up the so-called Watergate affair. Under threat of impeachment for his involvement and his repeated denials, Nixon resigned the presidency on August 9, 1974, the first U.S. president to do so. It was difficult for both Johnson and Nixon White House kids to watch and listen as so much of the country protested the actions of their fathers.

Gerald Ford, a longtime member of the House of Representatives, had been named vice president by Nixon after the elected vice president, Spiro Agnew, resigned in 1973. Now Ford became the only non-elected president in the nation's history.

When Gerald Ford took office, the youngest of the four Ford children, Susan, was a teenager. "I have good memories of the White House," she said in an interview for this book. "I was the only one to have my senior prom held there! It was great. I got to meet people and take trips." She admitted that after college she probably got some jobs as a photojournalist because she was a White House kid; but then, she said, "I had to prove myself."

Susan said that for a teenager, the White House is a cross between reform school and a convent. She remembered that the press made a big fuss because she wore jeans, which were not considered proper attire at that time. And dating was rough. "Imagine," she said, "how difficult it is when your date is greeted by the president of the United States!"

Yet Susan had a good time in the president's house. She reflected that "Perhaps my teen years weren't as

[78]

Gerald Ford
and daughter
Susan show off
the Fords'
golden retriever.
Susan caused a
stir by frequently
wearing jeans.

affected by the White House as some of the other kids'. After all, I grew up in Washington, D.C. When we moved into the White House, I didn't have to change schools or friends. As for the Secret Service, I also grew up with brothers, so the Secret Service didn't affect me either!''

Susan found living in the public eye the hardest when it was disclosed that her mother, Betty Warren Ford, had breast cancer. "That was difficult," she recalled, "to have the world looking in on you." She did not understand her mother's decision at the time to go public with the news, so that other women might be warned, but later Susan often lectured on how breast cancer affects a family.

Today, Susan Ford Bales lives with her husband and four children in Tulsa, Oklahoma. Brother Michael is on the faculty at Wake Forest University in North Carolina. Brother Jack, who used to raise eyebrows because he loved to party, owns shopping malls in San Diego, California. Brother Steve, a former rodeo cowboy and once a soap-opera star, now breeds horses on his ranch in California.

Amy Carter

As a young woman, Susan Ford felt very angry when her father lost the election of 1976 to James Earl (Jimmy) Carter. The thirty-ninth president and his wife, Rosalyn Smith, had four children. Chip, Jack, and Jeff were grown when their parents moved into the White House. Amy, nine years old, was the youngest White House kid since the Kennedys.

Amy was not a young lady eager for the press. She kept a cat named Misty Malarky Ying Yang and a low profile. Amy liked to sit in her tree house on the White House grounds reading and daydreaming. So it was with considerable surprise that, some years later, the American public heard that Amy Carter, a student at Brown University, had been arrested! In all, she was arrested four times in connection with student demonstrations. Amy left Brown, graduated from Memphis College of Art in 1991, and then went on to graduate school. She

[81]

continued to keep a low profile and avoid publicity. Scheduled to appear on the *Today* show in 1993 with other former White House kids, Amy Carter just didn't show up.

The Reagan and Bush Years

The White House family least troubled by an entrance into the spotlight surely has to be that of Ronald Wilson Reagan. Both the fortieth president and his wife, Nancy Davis, were motion picture actors before his election to the governorship of California and then the presidency.

The four Reagan children—Maureen, daughter of Reagan's first wife, Jane Wyman; Michael, who was adopted; Patty Davis; and Ron—were grown by inauguration day in 1981. None actually lived at 1600 Pennsylvania Avenue. Even though she was not a White House kid, Patty had a comment on her situation. "I think that you have to realize that there is nothing normal about being the child of a president of the United States. There are only a handful of people in the world who are ever going to experience this—and it is unique."

George, Jeb, Neil, Marvin, and Dorothy, children of George Herbert Walker Bush and his wife, Barbara Pierce, know that experience. They too were grown when Vice President Bush became the nation's forty-first president in 1989. Although the Bush sons and daughter were scattered from Texas to Colorado to Maine, the Bush White House was filled with the sounds of young people. George and Barbara Bush always enjoyed their grandchildren, all twelve of them.

During the four years of the Bush administration, there were numerous pictures of the president and First Lady romping with the White House grandchildren on the lawn or relaxing at their summer home in Kennebunkport, Maine. When George Bush lost the election to Bill Clinton in 1992, reporters asked him what his next business would be. He replied, "The grandpa business."

Chelsea Clinton

It's hard to say what caused the biggest stir when the Clintons moved into the White House in January 1993—how Socks, the First Cat, would adjust to his new surroundings, or whether Chelsea Clinton, twelve years old and the new White House kid, would go to public or private school.

From all reports, Socks, a bright-eyed, black-and-white feline of uncertain ancestry, adjusted quite well to public life. It is not known whether he has his own personal Secret Service guard. However, he is definitely Chelsea's cat—both her parents are allergic to him!

There were boos and cheers when William Jefferson and Hillary Rodham Clinton decided to send their only child to Sidwell Friends, a private school. The Carters had sent nine-year-old Amy to public school, but the Clintons felt that Chelsea's life was being turned upside down by the move to Washington and that a private school would shelter her from the glaring public spotlight. They probably had reason for concern, for when Chelsea heard the news of her father's election in 1992, she reportedly burst into tears. She was glad for her

father, but worried about such a big move. The choice of a private school seemed to help. Chelsea was seen on television at some White House functions or family outings, but the Clintons obviously wanted to keep their young daughter away from too much publicity.

One former president's daughter, Patty Davis, had some advice for incoming White House kid Chelsea Clinton: (1) Get your own refrigerator for your bedroom because they don't keep food in the upstairs kitchen. (2) Don't leave your Secret Service agents in the dust. It just makes them angry. (3) Find the secret passageways in the White House and use them to hide out sometimes. (4) Never pay attention to *anything* that anybody writes about you. (5) Above all, keep a sense of humor!

Opposite:
Arriving in
Washington
for her father's
inauguration
in 1993,
Chelsea Clinton,
12, waves to
photographers.

Conclusion:
"It Changes You Forever"

We can't ask a grown-up Maria Monroe or Jesse Grant how living in the White House changed their lives. But we did ask more recent White House kids. This is what some of them said.

More than anything, John Coolidge, nearly seventeen years old when his father became president in 1923, remembered being lonely living in the White House. "My brother and I had no friends. All my friends were in prep school and we had a hard time making new ones, just like any teenager who moves away from home. The White House was a formal, restricted place, and you don't just hang out somewhere and meet new people."

Julie Nixon Eisenhower was a young married college student living in the White House when her father was president from 1969 to 1974. "The White House is more fun the younger you are," she said. "Later it gets more difficult. And you never get used to the Secret Service. I thought the world was watching me as a newlywed and a college student.

[86]

"For a young person seeking independence, it's grim. You can't go to the drugstore, visit, have a fight in private. I found it oppressive and stiffling.

"Once you've been a White House kid, you'll always be a White House kid. It's always part of you. You'll always be so thought of even when you feel you're beyond it. You never get over such an experience, good or bad. Everything is compared to that experience before and after."

Said Susan Ford Bales, daughter of former President Gerald Ford, "It's not a whole lot of fun to be written about in the press every time you make a move. I had a tough time. Teenagers are considered fair game. I remember my mother saying, 'The children were not elected to this office. Leave them alone.' "

Perhaps the most telling comment about what it means to be a White House kid comes from the press office of Hillary Rodham Clinton, mother of Chelsea. Our request for an interview was politely refused, because her parents want Chelsea to live as normal a life as possible. Therefore, they say no to all requests for interviews, no matter how worthwhile the reason.

The spokeswoman added, "President and Mrs. Clinton don't want Chelsea in the spotlight or turned into a celebrity. They don't want her forever affected by being a member of the family of the president."

Yet, publicity or no publicity, Chelsea *will* be affected—just because she is a member of the family of the president. Like Susan Adams and Tad Lincoln, Julie Nixon Eisenhower and John Fitzgerald Kennedy, Jr., once a White House kid, always a White House kid.

[87]

Presidential Families

C = children
* = president's stepchild and/or adopted child
G = grandchildren who lived in the White House

1789–97   Washington, George and Martha Dandridge Custis
          (only presidential family not to live in the White House)
          C: Jacky*, Little Patt*
          G: Nelly, Little Wash

1797–1801 Adams, John and Abigail Smith
          C: Abigail, John, Charles, Thomas
          G: Susan

1801–09   Jefferson, Thomas and Martha Wayles Skelton
          C: Martha, Maria

1809–17   Madison, James and Dolley Payne Todd
          C: Payne Todd*

1817–25   Monroe, James and Elizabeth Kortright
          C: Eliza, Maria

1825–29   Adams, John Quincy and Louisa Catherine Johnson
           C: George, John, Charles Francis

1829–37   Jackson, Andrew and Rachel Donelson Robards
           C: Andrew Jackson, Jr.*

1837–41   Van Buren, Martin and Hannah Hoes
           C: Abraham, John, Martin, Smith

1841   Harrison, William Henry and Anna Symmes
           C: Elizabeth, John Cleves, Lucy, William Henry Jr., John
                 Scott, Benjamin, Mary, Carter, Ann
           G: William Henry III, James

1841–45   Tyler, John and Letitia Christian; Julia Gardner
           C: Mary, Robert, John Jr., Letitia, Elizabeth, Alice, Tazewell

1845–49   Polk, James Knox and Sarah Childress

1849–50   Taylor, Zachary and Margaret Smith
           C: Ann, Mary Elizabeth, Richard

1850–53   Fillmore, Millard and Abigail Powers; Caroline McIntosh
           C: Abigail, Powers

1853–57   Pierce, Franklin and Jane Means Appleton
           C: Benjamin

1857–61   Buchanan, James

1861–65   Lincoln, Abraham and Mary Todd
           C: Robert, Edward, William Wallace, Thomas

1865–69   Johnson, Andrew and Eliza McCardle
           C: Robert, Martha, Mary, Andrew Jr.
           G: Lillie, Andrew Patterson, Sarah, Mary, Andrew Stover

1869–77	Grant, Ulysses Simpson and Julia Dent
	C: Frederick, U.S. Jr., Ellen, Jesse
1877–81	Hayes, Rutherford Birchard and Lucy Webb
	C: Birchard, Webb, Rutherford, Fanny, Scott
1881	Garfield, James Abram and Lucretia Rudolph
	C: Harry, James, Mollie, Irvin, Abram
1881–85	Arthur, Chester Alan and Ellen Lewis Herndon
	C: Chester Alan Jr., Ellen
1885–89	Cleveland, Grover and Frances Folsom
	C: Ruth, Esther, Marion, Richard, Francis
1889–93	Harrison, Benjamin and Caroline Scott; Mary Dimmick
	C: Russell, Mary Scott, Elizabeth
	G: Benjamin (Baby McKee), Mary Lodge
1893–97	Cleveland, Grover (see 1885)
1897–1901	McKinley, William and Ida Saxton
1901–09	Roosevelt, Theodore and Alice H. Lee; Edith Kermit Carow
	C: Theodore Jr., Alice, Kermit, Ethel, Archibald, Quentin
1909–13	Taft, William Howard and Helen Herron
	C: Robert, Helen, Charles
1913–21	Wilson, Woodrow and Ellen Axson; Edith Bolling Galt
	C: Margaret, Jessie, Eleanor
1921–23	Harding, Warren Gamaliel and Florence Kling DeWolfe

1923–29   Coolidge, Calvin and Grace Ann Goodhue
           C: John, Calvin

1929–33   Hoover, Herbert Clark and Lou Henry
           C: Herbert J., Allan Henry
           G: Peggy, Peter

1933–45   Roosevelt, Franklin Delano and Anna Eleanor Roosevelt
           C: James, Anna, Elliott, Franklin Jr., John
           G: Eleanor, Curtis Jr., Johnny

1945–53   Truman, Harry S. and Elizabeth Wallace
           C: Margaret

1953–61   Eisenhower, Dwight David and Mamie Geneva Doud
           C: John Sheldon Doud
           G: Dwight David II, Barbara Anne, Susan Elaine

1961–63   Kennedy, John Fitzgerald and Jacqueline Lee Bouvier
           C: Caroline, John Jr.

1963–69   Johnson, Lyndon Baines and Claudia Taylor
           C: Luci Baines, Lynda Bird
           G: Lyndon

1969–74   Nixon, Richard Milhous and Thelma Patricia Ryan
           C: Tricia, Julie

1974–77   Ford, Gerald Rudolph and Elizabeth Boomer Warren
           C: Michael, Jack, Steve, Susan

1977–81   Carter, James Earl and Rosalynn Smith
           C: Chip, Jack, Jeff, Amy

1981–89   Reagan, Ronald Wilson and Jane Wyman; Nancy Davis
          C: Maureen, Michael, Patty Davis, Ronald Jr.

1989–93   Bush, George Herbert Walker and Barbara Pierce
          C: George, Jeb, Neil, Marvin, Dorothy

1993–   Clinton, William Jefferson and Hillary Rodham
          C: Chelsea

For Further Reading

Blue, Rose, and Corinne J. Naden. *Barbara Bush: First Lady.* Hillside, NJ: Enslow, 1991.

Graves, Charles P. *John F. Kennedy: New Frontiersman.* New York: Chelsea, 1992.

Krensky, Stephen. *George Washington: The Man Who Would Not Be King.* New York: Scholastic, 1991.

The Living White House, rev. ed. Washington, DC: White House Historical Association.

Sloate, Susan. *Abraham Lincoln: The Freedom President.* New York: Ballantine, 1989.

St. George, Judith. *The White House: Cornerstone of a Nation.* New York: Putnam, 1990.

Sullivan, George. *How the White House Really Works.* New York: Dutton, 1989.

Index

```
973        Blue, Rose.
BLU
           The White House
             kids.


                              020115013
$17.90
```

DATE			
NO 2 '95			
NO 22'95			
DEC 14			
JA 12'96